More MAKING THE GRADE · GRADE 2

EASY POPULAR PIECES FOR YOUNG PIANISTS. SELECTED AND ARRANGED BY LYNDA FRITH

GW00367209

Exclusive distributors:
Music Sales Limited
Newmarket Road, Bury St. Edmunds, Suffolk IP33 3YB.
This book © Copyright 1995 Chester Music
ISBN 0-7119-5051-2
Order No. CH61083
Cover design and typesetting by Pemberton & Whitefoord.
Printed in the United Kingdom by
Caligraving Limited, Thetford, Norfolk.

Chester Music

(A division of Music Sales Limited)
8/9 Frith Street, London W1V 5TZ.

INTRODUCTION

This collection of 14 popular tunes provides additional attractive teaching repertoire to complement the first books in MAKING THE GRADE. As with the previous books, the pieces have been carefully arranged and graded and the collection is made up of well-known material which pupils will enjoy. The standard of the pieces progresses to Associated Board Grade 2.

CONTENTS

WALKING IN THE AIR
(THEME FROM 'THE SNOWMAN')

by Howard Blake

Play the introductory bars and all similar bars as smoothly as possible, to give the feeling of gliding through the air.

Moderately ♩ = 104

SOMEWHERE OUT THERE

by James Horner, Barry Mann & Cynthia Weil

In bars 21 to 24 notice how the left hand mimics what the right hand has just played.

Try to bring out the left hand tune in these bars.

6

LOVE HURTS

by Boudleaux Bryant

Use the pedal very carefully in bars 17 to 24. Listen hard, making sure that the sound doesn't become 'smudgy'.

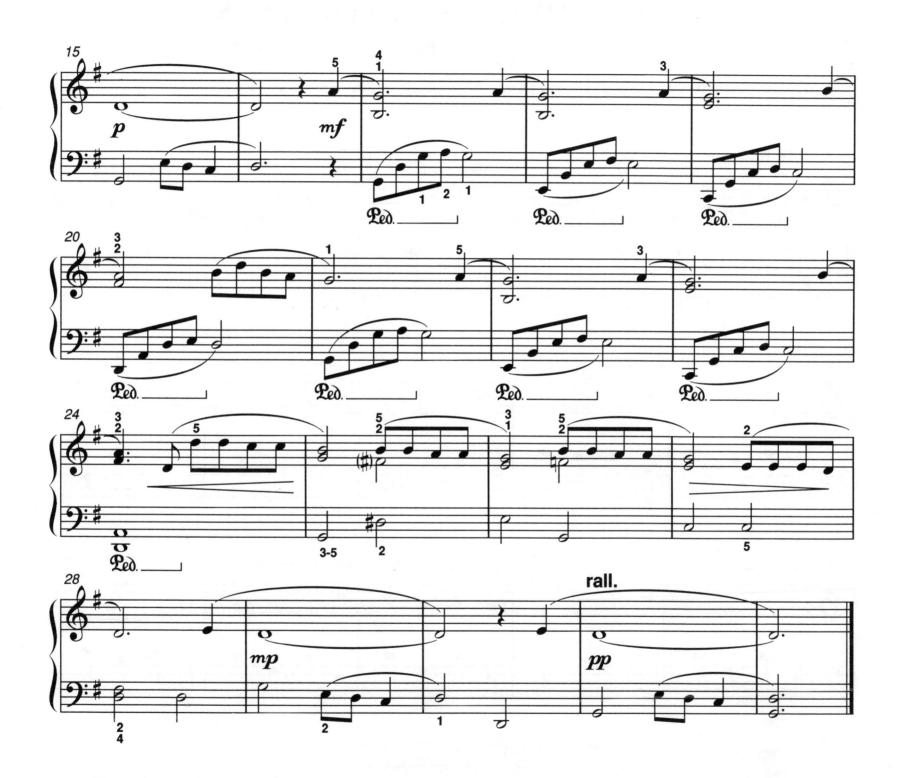

9

REVIEWING THE SITUATION

by Lionel Bart

The left hand is to be played very lightly, almost staccato, in order to create a feeling of humour.

A WHITER SHADE OF PALE

by Keith Reid & Gary Brooker

Avoid 'snatching' the pairs of semiquavers each time they occur, as the style of this piece is quite relaxed.

HE AIN'T HEAVY... HE'S MY BROTHER

by Bobby Scott & Bob Russell

In this piece the tune really needs to sing out. Try some gentle pedalling in bars 18 to 26.

MEMORY

by Andrew Lloyd Webber & Trevor Nunn (after T.S. Eliot)

Notice the time signature change in bar five; make sure that you keep the length of the quavers the same.

If you have difficulty thinking in $\frac{12}{8}$, try imagining the $\frac{12}{8}$ bars as two bars of $\frac{6}{8}$ to start with.

(The 'dotted' bar lines are there to help you with this.)

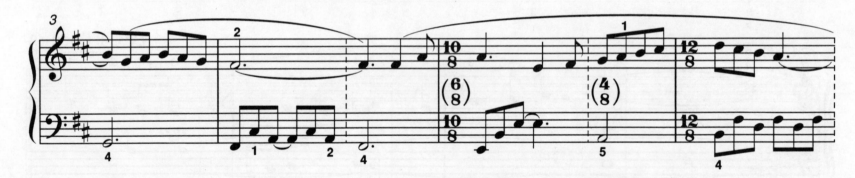

FIDDLER ON THE ROOF

by Jerry Bock & Sheldon Harnick

Play the left hand staccato throughout in contrast to the right hand, which needs to be sustained.

Be careful of the accidentals.

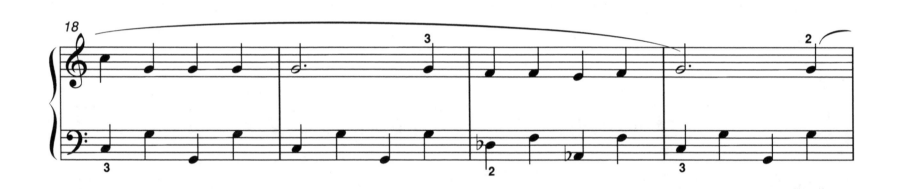

TOM TRAUBERT'S BLUES

by Tom Waits

Although subtitled 'Waltzing Matilda', notice that this piece is not written in waltz time!

ONE MOMENT IN TIME

by Albert Hammond & John Bettis

This piece starts very simply with a repetitive right hand rhythm. Put in plenty of expression to give interest and variety.

Quite slowly ♩ = 100

KING HEROD'S SONG

by Andrew Lloyd Webber & Tim Rice

This piece should move along quite briskly. You will need to practise slowly at first, and gradually increase the tempo.

D.C. al Coda

Coda

FERRY 'CROSS THE MERSEY

by Gerard Marsden

Try to feel the two minims in each bar as this will help you to play the triplets in time.

MONEY, MONEY, MONEY

by Benny Andersson & Bjorn Ulvaeus

There are many accents in bars 19 and 20. They change from being ON the beat to OFF the beat. Don't stop counting!

PENNY LANE

by John Lennon & Paul McCartney

The semiquavers in the Coda will need extra practice in order to play them up to speed. Notice the beat stays the same.

to Coda ⊕   D.S. al Coda ⊕

31

5/03 (47659)